Gordon Jar

Bessy Bell

and Bell

other Irish Intersections

Twenty-one poems old and new

To Victor — a real Irishman!
Best wishes from Gordon —
maybe an honorary one?

May 2013

Harper*croft* 2013

First published 2013 by
Harpercroft Books
24 Castle Street, Crail
Fife, Scotland KY10 3SH

*Minding a slew of inspirational teachers at Magee
University College, Derry (Alan Warner, Edwin
Rhodes, Ollie Edwards); and at Trinity College,
Dublin (W F Pyle, R B D French, J K Walton,
Frank O'Connor and Christopher Salvesen)*

Acknowledgement and thanks are due to editors
of the several journals which first supported
these poems by publishing them: *Acorn* (1962),
Ulster Graduate (1998), *Poetry Scotland* (2005),
Lallans (2009), *Fras* (2011), *Ullans* (2012), *The
Pathhead Review* (2012), *Reflexion No 7* (2012)
and *Northwords Now* (2013). Thanks are also due
to Owen Dudley Edwards, Tom Hubbard,
Hayden Murphy and Denis Stewart for advice
and editorial comments.

Pamphlet design by Mark Blackadder, Edinburgh
Printed by West Port, St Andrews

ISBN 978-0-9572014-1-5

Contents

Oh wad some power the giftie gie us
To see oursels as ithers see us!
It wad frae monie a blunder free us,
An' foolish notion . . .

Robert Burns, "To a Louse" (1786)

Ballast Bank, Troon

For James Anderson, first of my Irish friends

They told us Troon's coal-boats
used to return from Ireland empty
apart from a dark ballast of Irish soil.

The ballast became the town's Ballast Bank,
a raised plateau stretching half a mile
along the shoreline beside the harbour.

They told us this was the only place
in Scotland where wild shamrocks grew,
so we hunted for them as far as the sawmill.

We never found any, a childhood disappointment,
and we decided the soil wasn't Irish at all
but dredged instead from the adjacent harbour.

The Ballast Bank remains a vantage point
for spying flying washing lines to landward
and ships on the sea plying the Firth of Clyde.

It gives forby some shelter from fierce westerlies
whipping across the ocean; another Troon feature
being its trees all leaning sideways, drunk.

A teenager, I followed the Troon coal-boats
to attend university in Ireland. The Derry quays
had coal-yards along the Foyle, below the campus.

My room-mate's dad was a coal merchant
in The Diamond, Donegal. Troon's coal-boats
sailed there too . . . Imagine! Only connect.

Such links were all unlooked for
in my sheltered youthful Ayrshire world,
but I was well pleased by these connections.

Paddy's Milestone, 1960

Prelude and postscript

From Troon I travelled south by train
in early autumn all those years ago.
We passed by Paddy's Milestone
on the Firth of Clyde away to my right,
its lighthouse beam punctuating the night.

Passing that great stone lumpy outline,
I knew I'd soon be on the boat,
crossing the sea towards the rest of my life,
living by my own rules, my own best lights . . .
I was eighteen, couldn't get away fast enough.

Next sighting of it, now on the left,
came from a train window travelling north.
This time it signalled that in half an hour
I'd be home again for Christmas
to a place I had finally outgrown.

Paddy's Milestone is the rock of Ailsa Craig,
a hard granite place that once supplied the world
with curling stones; a marker light
for boats or travellers Erin-bound,
or in reverse for north-faring Irish folk.

Express trains fifty years ago had glamorous names:
"Flying Scotsman", "Royal Scot", "The Talisman" . . .
Our line from Glasgow to Stranraer Harbour
was where "The Paddy" ran to meet connections
with cross-Channel ferries to Larne. It was
the heyday of an integrated transport policy.

If the Fat Controller from *Thomas the Tank Engine*
had worked on this line, "The Paddy" was the train
for which he'd have sidelined all the others.

I did the same. "The Paddy" was my lifeline
between a life in two places, even if I only wanted
responsibilities in one. In the fullness of time
I grew up and accepted a few duties in both.

Crossing the Border, 1960

Driving out Northland Road
from Derry into Donegal
you had to stop at Customs then –
Muff or Bridgend.

A Customs officer nodded you through
in daylight hours. But after midnight
you dealt with sinister-looking boyos
in black uniforms, sometimes with guns.

A lot of the boyos had attitude,
expressions that said, "I dare you!"
I learned early about this, one night
in maybe my second Irish week.

Oh yes, I forgot to say
the Border closed then at about 2 a.m.
After that I think a barrier gate came down
or you were magicked into a purple banshee.

Anyway, on that post-midnight hour I drove
through a seemingly deserted checkpoint.
Away to my left a red light started swinging,
for all the world like a high-church censer.

I swerved, accelerating. Next thing,
they were firing shots at me, so – ever
a reasonable man – I stopped the car.
Words were exchanged. "Where the hell

do you think you're going?" barked boy
with gun. "Home to my bed," said I,
unaccustomed to gunfire or censers,
trying to ignore my wildly blinking eye.

A boring Q + A ensued, and that was that.
The following week a wee man in a dog-collar
invited me to join the B Specials, no less.
At least I now knew what they were.

But I declined his inexplicable proposal
while the Reverend gave me the eye.
Stiffly he told me I was now a marked man . . .
I know *that*, I thought. Interesting times.

Ballad of an Irish student

It fell upon the simmer-time
when the muir-men mak thir hay
that Donnie decided whit the hell,
he hud tae get away.

He'd been at the college nigh on a year,
he wis donnert an doit an cut,   *donnert*, dazed   *doit*, feeble
an if he didna get oot an aboot
he wis feart he'd dae his nut.

Ye can thole yer wurk fer hawf the year   *thole*, put up with
but then it sterts tae pall,
an it's yer duty tae jink it then   *jink*, dodge
an hiv yersel a ball.

Frae Derry Donnie crossed the sea
an hiked tae London toon.
But he sensed ould John Knox at his back
an he wantit tae act the loon.

Ye've cam thus faur, ye'd best gae on –
there's nae point sittin here,
waitin fer Godot, waitin, waitin,
waitin an drinkin beer.

Anither sea has tae be crossed
if ye're huntin fer the sun.
Ye're a bit lik a burd migrating
or a criminal on the run.

He pushed on south, a sun-worshipper,
something tellt him he must.
It hud sayd the same tae a wheen o fowk   *wheen*, heap
buried lang syne i the dust.

He left his pack at a hostelry
(a youth hostel, as fowk noo say),
an went tae work tae tread the grapes
in order tae earn some pey.

The vineyaird wis a sunny airt   *airt*, place
abune the Rhone's braid stream,   *abune*, above
an the wurkers sang as they pickit the fruit
an Donnie began tae dream . . .

o a better life i the open air
o a purpose lang fergot,
o mortality an apathy
an a' he hud been taught.

They supped in an ould French fairmhoose,
food an wine an mair;
they looked efter him weel at the fairmhoose,
they'd lost thir ain lad at the war.

The lass o the hoose wis Lili,
she wis wee an broon an hot,
an he thocht a lot aboot Lili,
an he thocht, "Aweel, how not?"

For mony a week Donnie bidit there,
an warsled ablow the sun   *warsled*, laboured
getting baked an stiff an derk an broon
in this, his hame fae hame.

But he hud tae move aff an see some mair,
the wanderlust tellt him again
loud an clear, "Ye've no much time."
So he thocht he'd gang tae Spain.

He gaed tae Madrid an Granada,
it gied him a sort o' a glow –
a twintieth-century pilgrim
wi nae place special tae go.

He spent a nicht in a monastery
tae mend his siller cord.
They tuik him in, brak breid wi him
an prayed until thir Lord.

The morn's morn he wis aff again   *the morn's morn*, next morning
fer they widna let Donnie stey.
But he gaed back intil thir chapel
an listened til them pray.

It wis on the road tae Toledo
that a Yankee crossed his trail,
a rich American pilgrim
who wis studying math at Yale.

His nem wis Joe, he seyd tae Don,
an could anyone tell a fella
the prettiest, quickest, mostest road
fae there tae Compostela?

Well, aff they gaed, the twae o them
an sune they wis guid pals,
fer Joe wis jist a simple sowl
wi a single interest: gals.

They tuik thir leave at Santander.
Joe wis heidit fer Rome,
but Donnie's time hud near rin oot
an he turned his feet fer home.

Three months hud relaxt wir freend here:
he wis a different man.
He cud face a winter at college
as weel as emdy can.

emdy, anybody

The boys they wir doon at Cassidy's Bar
drinkin the bluid-red wine
when Donnie Bain sailed up the Foyle
an stepped hame oot o the brine.

"Sure it's great tae see ye back ould man,
ye've been gone a quare lang time –
whitiver wis it tuik ye awa
an left us here tae a life o crime?"

Donnie shrugged, an sat in by the fire,
fer he couldna really say.
"Sure it's guid tae be back – a Guinness please,
I'll tell yez some ither day."

His motives belang tae anither tale,
tae a serious work in fact.
Ye'll no find here the Haly Grail
an leave an ould ballad intact.

Spring term, Magee College, Derry, 1962

The fairy thorn tree

For William Young

In those more innocent times
before the latest Troubles
I hitched to country places
like Dungiven.

On arrival, driven
to the very door – "No trouble, son" –
I am quizzed at length
about my driver. Would that
be Maguire the vet
or his brother Joe from up the Feeny road
by Knockan Bridge?
It isn't nosiness so much
as plain proof of country living
where everyone knows everyone
whatever their persuasion.

On the Saturday afternoon,
a sunny windy day,
the rector takes us shooting, his son and me.
To my surprise the man turns out
a dead-eye shot, and him a clergyman.
He bags as many snipe in half an hour
as I'd caught mackerel a month before
a mile out of Troon harbour with my dad.

Afterwards, striding across a blustery moor
behind a house called Pellipar he takes great pride
in showing me an ancient skeagh-bush –   *skeagh*, fairy
a squat and stunted little blackthorn tree
stuck in a shallow hollow
at the dead centre of nowhere,
but so decked out with bits of rag and cloth
that it appears a strange lost Christmas thing
beached on a summer strand.

Some of the rags are leprous and snot-green,
so it is not a thing of mystery
or beauty – rather just a scabby emblem
to a folk superstition
that still flourishes hereabouts
when nobody is looking.

Sunday turns out a busy day
for a country rector, even one
semi-retired "from active combat".
My host – surely in great demand? –
appears to spend his day driving about
to this or that outpost of his faith
for communion or evensong
or some other celebration.

I wonder idly if any of the churches
where he performs his mysteries
might have decked themselves out
as fervently and tastelessly
as that little fairy thorn tree.

Coda, 1983

Twentysomething years on
from that weekend in another country –
or was it in another world? –
I sit in the morning bustle of a street cafe
somewhere off London Piccadilly
sipping cappuccino while I make
urgent, last-minute preparations
for a strategic business meeting
of such paramount importance
that I've long forgotten what it was about.

Then, across that cafe's hum and two decades
I hear a voice I know – English vowels
in a swirl of Irish mist, and I recognise
the speech of my one-time school friend,
the Ulster rector's son. Hailing him, I say,
"You're a long way from the fairy thorn tree."

The startled head swings round to face me
with quickly dawning grin. "Och aye,"
he mimics in his best stage Scots,
"It has tae be, it cannae be ither
than ma ould freend Rabbie Burns,
the Ayrshire plooman." We shake hands.

One night in Dublin

Overheard on a city bus, 22 November 1963:
"Our little bit of grandeur is gone."

A cold and wintry snap,
a light frosting of snow
dusts the dozing town
under a prescient yellow moon.

On such evenings –
even on Fridays –
the warmth of the Reading Room
is almost an attraction
as I get stuck in
to my *Pilgrim's Progress*.

Tonight a muffled restlessness
disturbs the studious calm.
Is it me, hankering for a wild weekend
or is there something else?

Ten o'clock. A bell rings, so soon.
A tide of students
ebbs from the round room,
returns borrowed books
and seeps out into the white crispness
of Front Square.

I pause and light a cigarette.
A friend asks, through the gloom,
Did you hear? Hear what? I ask,
recalling the uneasy ripples
across the round Reading Room
and the knelling bell. A doom?

We talk, and then go separate ways.
I, in a blank daze,
enter a pub to watch it all
on a merciless blue screen
high on a bar-room wall.
Old Bartkus buys me a beer.
I sip at it; I try to take this story in.

From Vanity Fair,
beyond Doubting Castle
and across the River of Death,
with all his marks and scars
Mr President has today passed over.
Today the trumpets sounded for him
upon the other side.

Looking around this room
I read one questing thought
on every silent face and taut
now he is gone from Camelot:
Who will fight Giant Despair for us now
and help us through this dark shadow?

Postscript, 31 August 1997

This poem happened many years ago
as I began to weigh the passing years.
It describes a spasm of my world's soul
even farther back in time. It is
a yellowing snapshot of a young man's tears.

A life's defining moments don't recede. Today
is a sunny summer morning thirty-four years on
from that far-off distress. An older man
and world wake up to learn
of another violent death.

This death of a princess is a strange demise.
A chauffeur-driven butterfly caught in a gyre
has flown inexorably at a funeral pyre
of her own creation, intoxicated
on the oxygen of her own publicity,
an accident dying to happen,
hoist on its own petard.

Another of their mother's photo opportunities,
I pity her poor children now bereft. I pity too
an older generation impelled to remember
a cold and wintry night in November
so very long ago.

Rue Duhesme

For Tommy Murtagh, one-time classmate

A suburban Paris street, grubby flats that slope
down the steep back of the Butte Montmartre
past the Hôtel de Ville of the 18th arrondissement
towards Rue Ornano and the Marché aux Puces.
A good working-class area, says the concièrge
with garlic-flavoured cackle and weary warcry
of *Liberté, égalité, fraternité,*
nous couperons le gaz et l'électricité !

Mornings, a busy pungent Métro ride away
to L'Odéon from Marcadet-Poissonniers,
for French literature classes at the Sorbonne –
the great Etiemble playing to packed houses
on the poetry of Rimbaud and the significance
of his "Voyelles" in the dusty busty pantheon
of great Frenchmen. One day, shall I tell you
their latent possibilities? One day . . .

Afternoons, the brisk walks up Rue Caulaincourt,
conversation classes at Lycée Janson de Sailly
with raucous youths, *la jeunesse insolente*.
Later, in the early evenings I dawdle back
to nameless street cafés round Place Clichy
for further conversation, this time with ladies
of the night: earnest discussion about *les clients*
and the various services they demand. I learn
about the annual depreciation – for tax purposes,
you understand – of a state-registered prostitute,
and about the hazards of the oldest profession . . .
Don't ask too much about where I learned my French.

The evening promenade past piquant cooking smells,
yellow-lit window shapes in blocks of black stone
under a toenail moon, a souvenir of inky sky: while I
silently declaim a poem to suit the mood of my day,
walking in step to its rhythms. Do my lips move?
Do folk nudge one another and chuckling, say,
Regardez monsieur qui parle tout seul ? No matter.
Je suis le Ténébreux, le Veuf, l'Inconsolé –
I am the shadowy, solitary, inconsolable one,
the disinherited prince of the roofless tower,
his lodestar burnt out, his wounded lute
playing only dark and melancholy tunes today.

Home to my studies, essays, sometimes
to a visit from the landlord – elderly, gay,
a Breton nationalist and novelist *manqué*,
usually well soused in aftershave and brandy
in equal measures. He's okay,
seriously repulsive, hardly a threat
to anyone's celibacy, another disinherited prince
with no one to hear him and far too much to say.

Student posers snagged

Monkstown, Co Dublin, 1963

Mid-Victorian villas front Belgrave Square,
flat-roofed and grey but handsome of their kind.
For a single magic spell we linger there to find
ourselves, oblivious to the neighbours' sidelong glare.

Respectable locals walk the dog, troop off to Mass,
hurry down to the train, up to commuter bus,
uncomfortable with this intrusive pair
contaminating their genteel salt-sea air.

We sprawl around in early summer sun
under the clipped trees on that well-cut grass,
making half-hearted stabs at reading the set texts,
preparing essays for Mademoiselle Rollin

or the next tutorial for Dr Pyle. But mainly we
submerge ourselves in one another's company,
me gagging for an ebullient encore to yesterday,
snagged on a sassy siren's lure once more.

Miss Murphy goes to business in the town
and Father Kelly comes to Sunday lunch.
The face of Mrs Corbett wears its ever-wintry frown.
Fatuously infatuated we ignore the whole suburban bunch.

Seventy years on, *or* What then?

After "What Then?", a late W B Yeats poem commissioned by Derry Jeffares for first publication in Dublin High School's magazine, The Erasmian, *April 1937*

He worked to get a good degree at college,
he wrote some stuff for cash and made true friends,
and though the world was often too much with him,
he tried to put the means before the ends.
    "What then?" sang Plato's ghost, "What then?"

He roamed the world from Chile to Nigeria,
he scaled the hills of Scotland one by one,
he took his share of pleasures where he found them
and had his little portion in the sun.
    "What then?" sang Plato's ghost, "What then?"

Like Willie Yeats, his happier dreams came true:
a small old house, wife, daughter, son,
a flower garden where birds sang and flew,
good friends to come for visits – many a one.
    "What then?" sang Plato's ghost, "What then?"

In age he wondered if the work went on
or if already he'd run out of time.
He watched his plans unravel with the seasons
and in the sands he started to draw his line.
    While louder sang that ghost, "What then?"

2007

A neighbour's death

Derry Jeffares, 1920–2005

I went to the newspaper as is my wont
to read the poem of the day,
but didn't yesterday. Instead I saw
his striking photograph and the obituary.

The photo captured a whiff of his spirit –
wise, generous, sparky, convivial.
News of his death, whom I'd met so lately
arrested all my working day.

I wish we'd had more time
to discuss matters of mutual curiosity:
Crail, Yeats and Dublin for a start
and the whole business of making poetry.

Knowing him so briefly I had no expectancy
to hear in dream his Irish voice address me,
conversing in that gossipy, gleeful way
I'd so enjoyed at supper recently.

Will we imagine conversations like this
in times to come? The dead we miss
are easier to talk to, someone said;
which may be true, albeit sad.

I'm sure his death has intervened
in many lives. We who go on a while
will carry him along. Meanwhile,
I've still not read the poem of the day.

Dublin weekend

For Frances, companion through time and space

Both of us being Edinburgh born and raised
I'm sorry it took us thirtysomething years
before I got to show you bits of my Dublin.

But now at last together we've walked a Liffey quay
or three, inspected riverside boardwalks new to me
and agreed the traffic reminds us of gay Paree.

I always liked the human Liffey bridges
named for people plucked from Irish history:
Butt, O'Connell, Grattan, Father Mathew –
each with its resonance, none more sonorous
than O'Donovan Rossa. These old friends
now jostle with newer crossings: Millennium Bridge,
Sean O'Casey Bridge (Polish-built, says the plaque),
Matt Talbot Bridge . . . This town is prospering.

Trinity College has weathered well since my time,
but we give up on the Book of Kells till tomorrow.
Today's queue stretches round Fellows' Square,
a new feature since I was there.

Next day we're thwarted too: a state visit this time
by the Slovak president plus entourage of big black cars
has closed the place to *hoi polloi* like us.

The following day we're third-time lucky: we get
to jostle and peer at scripts from medieval books
and gape at the soaring Long Room shelves.

Later: sober memorial to a terrible beauty,
the GPO looks smart and well maintained
amid the tat and hurly-burly of O'Connell Street.

The portico and domed rotunda of City Hall
and the squares and towers of Dublin Castle
are more echoic, more atmospheric than I recall.

The Central Bank's a new kid on the block
in Dame Street: discreet bunker for the gnomes
of Dublin, punchy powerhouse of the Celtic tiger?

Strongbow's effigy still pulls a curious crowd
into Christ Church, whose other draws include
a spooky crypt, memorials in stone and brass,
colourful floor-tiles, finest stained glass,
uplifting choral music of a once-ruling class.

You express surprise at the huge, majestic scale
of so many gracious eighteenth-century buildings:
the Custom House, Four Courts, Bank of Ireland,
Leinster House . . . "Built to keep the natives cowed
and in their place," says Tommy, Dublin-born and bred.
Then, laconic: "It worked for a while," he said.

Special visits: a good browse in Eason's Bookshop
and Hodges Figgis. How come they manage here
to support huge local booksellers, unlike us Scots?
How come a Penguin office in St Stephen's Green?

A quick DART out to the harbourside at Howth
and back in time for supper in O'Neill's Bar,
comforting timewarp from my long-gone youth.
No curates for barmen now – today's are Czech.

I enjoyed our trip, and hope we'll soon come back.
I know there's so much more to see, to show us
(if we want it) how our Scotland might be . . .

We'll walk in Merrion Square and Stephen's Green,
DART out by train to Dalkey and the Sugarloaf,
visit Aras an Uachtarain, explore a bit of Phoenix Park,
steer clear of noisy Temple Bar at weekends after dark . . .

I lived here once upon a day. I'd hoped to stay.
But then we'd not have met each other
and I might have lost my way.

April 2007

Coming back to Derry

Homage to John Frederick Kelly, 1905–1955

We travel to Derry by car and boat,
your daughter and I. I'm here for a college reunion
fifty years on. Frances is making her first-ever trip
to see the family home where you were born
and spent your formative early years.

Once we've found the house, we try to imagine you
on the steep-sloping terrace at 7 Marlborough Avenue:
a small Edwardian child with two big sisters
who like to mother you. We take some photos
to refresh the memory bank in case we don't return.

Tonight I read the poetry book your granddaughter gave me,
then phone to tell her and her brother our good news:
"We've seen the house," we tell them, "the hillside terrace,
the painted house-fronts, more colourful than Scotland."

Fred, you were the grandparent our children never knew,
you died so long ago. Your presence was an absence –
a bit exotic, a dead Irishman – in our prosy Scots household.
Now, at last, we've maybe got you into better view.

2010

At Quigley's Point, Lough Swilly

Beside the causeway's landward end
we look towards Inch Island.
I once learned to water-ski inexpertly
across this chilly arm of dark Lough Swilly.

From here, right up the bay to Fahan pier
a rubber wetsuit kept me just above freezing
until we ran chit-chittering into the Tower Bar
for beer and warmth and inner cheer.

Grianan of Aileach still stands sentinel here,
a look-out hillfort on the heights above the lough:
prehistoric man imbibed this magic view.
Today we stand here and survey it too.

2010

Snow

Today's snow puts me in mind of Miss Lindsay.
Fifty years ago she was my Derry landlady
and thought I was the child she'd never had.
I used to clear the pavements round her house,
retrieve her garden paths before they whited out,
help her with shopping, stuff like that.

She was a local worthy, ex-headmistress,
living in retirement – just as I now do.
She'd run a "good" school with flair and skill,
lived in a big brick house on Lawrence Hill,
and took in "good" students, which – being Ulster,
being her, being then – meant Presbyterians.
A Scotsman, I could in her eyes do no wrong
until one day she asked me my persuasion.

Pausing, I looked at her then at the floor,
mumbling I was a churchgoing atheist – no more.
Well, the nose turned snow-white as she squinted at me,
then exited the living room and slammed the door.
Later, there came the formal note. I had to go.
So ends this vignette called Miss Lindsay, OBE.

2010

Bessy Bell and Mary Gray:
An ould ballant concludit

*For John Herdman, of Perth; and minding Claud, Barbara
and Celia Herdman, of Sion Mills, Co Tyrone; forby Alan
Warner, sometime professor of English at Magee University
College, Derry. In 1961, Alan introduced me to Pairt I of this
poem, and first set this hare running.*

Pairt I: The fragment *(c.1610)*

O Bessy Bell and Mary Gray,
they war twa bonnie lasses.
They biggit a bower on yon burn-brae   *biggit,* built
and theekit it o'er wi rashes.   *theekit,* thatched   *rashes,* rushes

They theekit it o'er wi rashes green,
they theekit it o'er wi heather.
But the plague cam there wi Mary's man
an slew a' three thegethir.

They thocht tae lye neist Methven kirk
amang thir noble kin.
But noo they lye in Stronach pairk
to pey the price o sin.

O Bessy Bell and Mary Gray,
they war twa bonnie lasses.
They biggit a bower on yon burn-brae
and theekit it o'er wi rashes.

Pairt II: Dénouement *(2010)*

Noo Bessy'd hud a man forby   *forby,* as well, also
and left him brukkin-hertit.   *brukkin-hertit,* broken-hearted
Tae braw Strathearn he said guid-bye.
Fer Ulster he depairtit.

Fer undertaker tae Tyrone
his uncle John hud gaed.
He scrievit his nephew tae win on   *scrievit*, wrote
wi biggin a mill tae aid.

King Jamie sat upon his throne,
a-ruling kingdoms thrie,
a-planting prodestans athort Tyrone,   *athort*, across
as the lad noo sailed the sea.

wir younker, our youngster

Wir younker miller makkit a life   *makkit*, made
at the aits neist Sion Mills.   *aits*, oats   *neist*, next
He taen tae wad an Irish wife   *taen*, took   *wad*, wed
amang Tyrone's braw hills.

Twa nemless hills, o strange tae tell
he'd trevel monie a day.
He ca'd the first hill Bessy Bell
and the tither Mary Gray.   *the tither*, the other

Yon's thir nems richt tae this day   *nems*, names
forenent the vale o Strule,   *forenent*, opposite, facing
nems gien by a lad frae ower the sey   *sey*, sea (Ulster)
tae mind him o his dule.   *dule*, bereavement, loss

Note. The first part of the ballad is thought to date from the early to mid-17th century. It contains small detail apart from the names of the two ladies. They were supposed to have fled the town of Perth, where the plague raged, for a safe haven in the countryside around Strathearn or Glenalmond. But when Mary Gray's lover visited them in secret, he brought the plague from the town, and soon all three of them were dead.

The second part of the ballad assumes Bessy's lover to have been the sole grieving survivor of the two couples, and tells the story of how two hills in West Tyrone took the names of two dead 17th-century Perthshire girls. "Undertakers" at that time "undertook" to settle Protestant farm labourers and cottars in parts of Ulster during the Plantation, which started before 1610. Bessy Bell (1387ft) was the first Irish hill I ever climbed. Looking north-east, it faces across the vale of Strule to the lower summit still today called Mary Gray (828ft). In many ways, it is a landscape reminiscent of Perthshire.

Bessy Bell today has two other claims to fame. Alan Warner included its summit in his book *Walking the Ulster Way: A Journal and a Guide* (1989), referring to it in his poem "A Song of the Ulster Way" thus:

I took a walk in Ulster,
The Way is long to tell.
I went by Fairy Water
And over Bessy Bell . . .

Past Ballygawley Water
I walked to Auchnacloy,
I went by Legatillida,
By Maghery and Moy.

By Ramaket and Ballynure,
Drumgruff and Quiggy Hill,
By Pettigoe and Swanlinbar,
Drumlee and Columbcille . . .

All these were on the way I went,
Their names spelt out my track,
And still their echo haunts my mind
As I lay down my pack.

Nowadays the hill is climbed by many long-distance trekkers as they follow Alan's guide-book footpath. Bessy Bell is also said to have been an inspiration for Mrs Cecil Frances Alexander (1818–95), author of the well-known Victorian hymn "All things bright and beautiful". She once lived near the hill. The words of verse 3 of the hymn begin: "The purple-headed mountain, the river running by . . ." It was said that this was a reference to the hill called Bessy Bell.

For more background information on this poem, see short article "Bessy Bell and Mary Gray: an ould Scots ballad fragment wi a new Ulster conclusion", in *Ullans* (Nummer 12, Wunter 2011/12, pp50–54).

Withering into the truth

After "The Coming of Wisdom with Time" (1910),
by W B Yeats

From wartime beginnings in seaside sun,
from all the weft and warp of my youth,
a lifetime's fabric is woven and done
now I'm weathering, withering into the truth.

I've had plenteous portions of joy and good fun;
a few regrets also, forby and forsooth.
Now behind the hill wilts a watery sun:
I am weathering, withering into the truth.

There dawns a sense that the race is run,
while loud and clear sounds the thundering hoof
of the galloping horse we once learned to shun.
I am weathering, withering into the truth.

The Apocalypse horse is a beast to shun
when we're weathering, withering into the truth.

2011

Railway waiting room, Dundalk

For Felicity Hayes-McCoy, John McArdle, Sam McBratney
and 'Gerard Woulfe', co-authors of Storyline Ireland *(1988),*
a project which gave me an excuse to make two trips to
Ireland.

From an empty upstairs waiting room
I listened for the Dublin express train
one sunny autumn afternoon.

Soon I was jumping into a carriage,
finding a window seat, and taking
a file of notes from an overnight bag.

I had an agenda to fine-tune
for a pre-planned two-day meeting
in Dublin the following morning.

Ah, but where were my spectacles?
Not in my luggage, nor about my person . . .
Panic quickly set in, as she does.

Instantly I knew it, the specs were in Dundalk –
how now to organise a meeting? The inspector
phoned ahead to see what could be done.

Arrived in Dublin, his colleague in the signals room,
all smiles, said the specs had been retrieved
and would be sent down by the evening train.

"Come back tomorrow morning," he said.
"I should have them here for you by then.
This is the railway with the personal touch."

Next day I got my specs back, and I knew
we'd have a good meeting. So the project
went forward, my Irish fates a-smiling.

Four days in Kerry

For Steven Fallon, most reliable of climbing mentors

I: Brandon Mountain *(13 July 2002)*

Exceptional weather. An Aegean blue
from Smerwick harbour hurts the eyes; the Dingle Way
jinks in and out of view around the bay.

The old cart-track of the Saint's Road climbs steadily,
marked out with cairns and white crosses,
guiding us through mosses and a cloud inversion

to emerge on the rocky lump called Brandon Mountain,
with views to the long eastward curve of Brandon Bay
and an open moor slanting up towards Brandon Peak.

The Pilgrim's Route looks a challenging scramble.
Tomorrow two questing souls may clamber
past dewy fuschia hedges to do a closer appraisal.

II: Macgillycuddy's Reeks, Part 1 *(14 July 2002)*

Today is misty so we tackle Carrauntoohil
from the east, leaving the car at Kate Kearney's cottage,
where a parking fee is charged: nice little earner.

The route follows Hag's Glen and the Devil's Ladder,
a warning coincidence of spooky names in slapping fog.
All the way up a wet wind taunts with wreaths of mist,
and almost to the summit of Ireland's highest hill
there's virtually no view, boo-hoo.

Then clouds lift here and there. We begin to see
bits of where we've been, bits of the horseshoe
we're headed to. The knife-edge ridge and stacks
of Knocknapeesta look like a good scramble,
so we pick out a route along the jagged scree.

Too soon we're on Cruach Mhor, our final rocky top
complete with holy niche and grotto to guide us
safely off the hill, back down into Hag's Glen.

III: Interval *(15 July 2002)*

A day off, easy
to slip into tourist mode
west along the long arm
of the Beara Peninsula,
across the Destitution Road
and down to little villages
with great big names
like Castletown Berehaven,
complete with gift shops
and harbour coffee bars.

Later, at Beara's end
we gaze over the water
to the little fields on Dursey Island
with its swinging cable car
slung low across a choppy strait.
We are tempted to go over.
But no, we're here for the hills –
so we leave Dursey for another day,
Dursey unvisited.

IV: Macgillycuddy's Reeks, Part 2 *(16 July 2002)*

The western horseshoe of the famous Reeks
is a splendid arc of linking tops and three main peaks.
Dame Fortune smiles down on a flawless Kerry day,
sunny and breezy. From Skregmore to Caher,
scrambling Beenkeragh's boulders and jagged arête
we take life easy, we enjoy it all the way.

For the second time in three days
we clamber onto Carrauntoohil's peak
rejoicing at today's clement weather,
at long, peerless views in all directions.

I got my first Irish "Munros" in 1962 –
the Wicklows and the lonesome Galtymore.
Today on Caher I've climbed my last.
Forty years a-questing, but what's the hurry?

Other Irish gems down the long years
illuminate a winding road. They include
two Slieve Snaghts in Co Donegal,
forby the fine twins of Muckish and Errigal;
the two Tyrone sisters Bessy Bell and Mary Gray;
Sligo's bold Ben Bulben one fine and windy day.

Concentrating, I smile to contemplate a roll-call
of hills that stretch across a life. I mind them all.

Note. "Munros" is a Scottish term referring to the 280+ separate hills of
Scotland that stand over 3000 feet (or 914 metres) in height. There is also a
scatter of "Furths" (Munros beyond Scotland) across the other nations of the
British Isles – 4 in England, 7 in Ireland and 8 in Wales – to attract aficionados
of the high hills. Hence the 2002 expedition.

A cold eye

A view from Ben Bulben's plateau, minding WBY

A cold eye surveyed the turning world today
just as it watched yesterday and yesterday.
Bagpipes below Ben Bulben blew and skirled
as all the wings on the host of the air unfurled
and all the world's wild elements piped away.

When first I came as pilgrim to Drumcliff
the poet occupied his narrow grave alone. Today
and ever after his Georgie keeps him company,
here in the poet's country of the heart –
by the lake of Innisfree and the hills above Glencar.

From here the rag-and-bone shop trundled far,
learning, deepening, burnishing the Yeatsean art.
To this druid place his heart was firm and true,
where faeries danced to a weird druidic tune
under magic stars and a faerie moon.

A County Sligo bell tolls for a youthful heart
here in Sleuth Wood and at farthest Rosses,
at Cummen Strand and Lissadell,
by Knocknarea and Dromahair's spell,
amid keening from Inishmurray in the bay.

No names, no pack drill,
or The famous poet

If I name-dropped, everyone would ask
the same questions: "What was he like?"
or, "Was he really in your year?"

So I'd backtrack, parry, play for time.
"Hell, it was years and years ago.
I don't remember him too well."

I conceded he was a bit of a scruff,
as most of us were in those days,
even staff like McDowell, the junior dean –

looking for all the world like a wayward scarecrow
flapping his ragged way across Front Square,
checking the policies, peering here and there.

The famous poet favoured a thick sweater
even if it made him appear slightly fat
because of the lumpy way it sat.

Once a week, four or five of us
might dine at a greasy spoon in Drury Street
or Suffolk Street under a bilious moon.

My sharpest recollection of the famous poet
was the night of the Ireland–Scotland rugby game
when afterwards we threw a party for the Scots.

Famous wee poet – all of five foot six – was addressed
by Peter Brown, Scottish captain, fully six foot six.
Little and Large argued, looked each other up and down.

Warming to his point, Brown (a gentle giant from Troon)
punched a large hole through my ceiling, thereby
admitting starlight and moonlight into the living room.

Famous poet looked round, rolled his eyes at me, intoned
with all the self-righteousness at his command, "First of all,
that act of vandalism was not mine: I couldn't reach

that ceiling if I tried. And secondly, Big Man,
be so good as to fetch me a fresh Guinness
since this one now has ceiling plaster floating in it."

Note. The game at Lansdowne Road in the spring of 1964 was hard fought and
won by Scotland 6–3, so Brown was a hero of the hour. But imagine the scandal
today if a visiting team captain and another player absented themselves post-
match even for an hour to go and relax with friends! Those were the good old
days of the amateur game.

In Hibernia Antiqua, *or* Tir nan Og

After Hilaire Belloc

Do you remember, Miranda, when the hiker at the lonely B&B
was charged one and sixpence for his breakfast and high tea
as he walked the Connemara coastline in 1963?

Do you remember when a bottle of Guinness
(price: eleven old pence) was thrown in for a nightcap?
"Drink it down now, and it'll give you a right good nap."

When a chipped cupful of rawest firewater poteen
induced a heavy dream-filled sleep of eighteen
lost hours, snug in an ancient armchair by the fire?

When your host refused to speak in the *English*
in case you turned out to be a spy from Dublin Castle
come to check your farmer host was using his *Irish* –

for which they paid him a welcome Gaeltacht grant?
Or are these just tall stories from the olden times,
à la Marco Polo, Mandeville et al? I wonder.

Notes on the poems

The majority of these poems were not written as (or for) an Irish collection, nor have they previously been presented together as an entity. They are a series of Irish excavations from a Scots memory bank, "occasional" poems blending poetry and memoir, written over a fifty-year timespan. The five books in which the earlier texts were collected in print (all published by Harpercroft) are shown in italics below. The eight most recent poems are marked "uncollected", and were written during 2012–13. Three are positioned at the beginning and five at the end of this collection, to serve as book-ends for the older texts.

1. "Ballast Bank, Troon", uncollected
2. "Paddy's Milestone, 1960: Prelude and postscript", uncollected
3. "Crossing the Border, 1960", uncollected
4. "Ballad of an Irish student", in *Now and Then Poetry and an Ould Ballad* (*NTP*, 2010)
5. "The fairy thorn tree", in *Ayrshire Recessional* (*AR*, 1998)
6. "One night in Dublin", in *AR*
7. "Rue Duhesme", in *NTP*
8. "Student posers snagged", in *NTP*
9. "Seventy years on, *or* What then?", in *Watching the Sun* (*WS*, 2008)
10. "A neighbour's death", in *The Tale of the Crail Whale* (*TCW*, 2006)
11. "Dublin weekend", in *WS*
12. "Coming back to Derry", in *Withering into the Truth* (*WIT*, 2012)
13. "At Quigley's Point, Lough Swilly", in *WIT*
14. "Snow", in *WIT*
15. "Bessy Bell and Mary Gray: An ould ballant concludit", in *WIT*
16. "Withering into the truth", in *WIT*
17. "Railway waiting room, Dundalk", uncollected
18. "Four days in Kerry", uncollected
19. "A cold eye", uncollected
20. "No names, no pack drill, *or* The famous poet", uncollected
21. "In Hibernia Antiqua, *or* Tir nan Og", uncollected

The first two poems were written after a rare 2012 visit to Troon, the Ayrshire town where I grew up. Poems 3–8 are all set during student days (1960–4) at either Magee University College, Derry, or at Trinity College, Dublin; with poem 7 something of an interloper, covering as it does a term of my third-year studies spent at the Sorbonne in Paris – because my degree subjects included French. "Ballad of an Irish student" (poem 4) is my first and oldest extant published poem, unusual here for being contemporaneously written, originally commissioned for Magee's student magazine, *Acorn*, at the instigation of my professor of English, Alan Warner. A copy of the 1962 poem was retrieved from the Magee library archives in 2010, Magee's records being far more meticulous than mine.

I began my undergraduate studies at Magee partly on the strength of a Martha Magee scholarship, for which I remain indebted. Incredible as it may sound nowadays, in 1960 I was Alan Warner's solo first-year honors English student. The teaching I received from him during my two freshman years was tailor-made and, perhaps as a result, inspirational. As part of my four-year study course, Alan treated me to a thorough overview of the ballad as a literary form: hence poems 4 and 15. Poems 5, 6, 7 and 8 marinated until the early or mid-1990s before they got written: student poems written after a 30-year gestation. Poems 9 and 10, "Seventy years on" and "A neighbour's death" are my Derry Jeffares poems, triggered as they were by the death in 2005 of my wonderful Irish neighbour (and W B Yeats scholar) at Fife Ness. "Seventy years on" is a poem after a Yeats original; as likewise is poem 16, "Withering into the truth". Yeats has been my favourite poet since student days. Bad teachers are said to kill poetry for their students; but several of my English teachers at Magee and at Trinity were exceptional, so it is almost certainly to their insights and enthusiasms that I owe an undimmed love of Yeats.

Poems 11 to 15 came about following two trips with my wife back down memory lane – by this date rather a long and winding road. The first visit was to Dublin in 2007, and the second to Derry in 2010. Poem 15 has had by far and away the longest gestation of any of my poetic perpetrations – a mere fifty years! I acknowledge in its dedication that it owes much to the long-ago balladic promptings of Professor Warner at Magee. Additionally, poem 4 resembles poem 15 in that both these ballads are written in versions of Scots – Scots-lite and Ullans – rather than standard English. Some glossaries are supplied.

Poem 17 is a story from my working life as a textbook publisher in the 1980s, poem 18 is a late hill poem, and 19 is perhaps my final nod in the direction of WBY; these last two poems both derived from a memorable climbing expedition into the hills of Co Kerry in the summer of 2002. Poems 20 and 21 are two late and light-hearted springtime postscripts, written just before this project was consigned to print (March 2013).

Gordon

To Sue
with .
Gordon Jarvie
Crail 2012.

Out
and
About
Poetry
Mainly from the
East Neuk, Fife

Harper*croft* 2012

Published 2012 by Harpercroft Books,
24 Castle Street, Crail, Fife KY10 3SH

First edition 2007, titled *Poems Mainly from the
East Neuk, Fife*, published by Akros, Kirkcaldy

For Frances; and minding Duncan Glen

Foreword and acknowledgements
These poems were written between 2003 and 2011,
and are arranged more or less chronologically. So
the back-story is about time passing, retirement,
and adapting from city life (in Edinburgh) into the
slow lane of rural Fife. Five of the later texts are
written in Scots.

The poems originally appeared in six short
pamphlets published by Harpercroft, as shown on
the contents list opposite. Some were also published
in *Fringe of Gold: The Fife Anthology* (ed. Duncan
Glen and Tom Hubbard, Birlinn, 2008) and *Skein
of Geese: Poems from the 100 Poets Gathering*
(ed. Eleanor Livingstone, StAnza, 2008); as well as
newspapers and magazines including *Fras, The
Herald, Lallans, Loose Scree, Markings, NorthWords
Now, Poetry Scotland, St Andrews in Focus, The
Red Wheelbarrow* and *Zed₂O*: the editorial
encouragement of all these publications is
acknowledged with thanks. The author is also
grateful to Lesley Duncan for several useful textual
suggestions; and, not least, he acknowledges a
Fife Culture Grant towards the cost of producing
this pamphlet.

Pamphlet design: Mark Blackadder, Edinburgh
Printer: West Port, St Andrews

ISBN 978-0-9572014-0-8

Contents

Moving to Fife: a sain

Me and the wife
have flitted to Fife
to live the life
    of Riley

With spade and pail
we've come to Crail
to tell a new tale
    entirely

Here's room for a rhyme
from time to time –
and that's no crime
    in poetry

A horizon of sea
encourages me
(like Hamlet) to *be* –
    quite simply

At sixty-two
there's much to do –
we'll try to do it
    wisely

We thank you God
so far so good
for health and food
    and family

And so we pray
keep us this way
through every day
    in safety

Another working Monday

I open sleepy shutters
to spy a sleek black cat
sauntering up the pavement opposite.
It pauses this sunny morning
to watch a sparrow and a starling
on the high garden wall
beside the apple tree.

"Hardly worth the effort,"
cat seems to say and then
continues along its way,
engrossed in whatever it is.

My lucky day?

7 p.m.

Home again. Another day at the office:
the place where tails wag dogs,
procedures dictate outcomes,
form blights substance,
and communication has lost out
to the babble of jargon –
the whole sclerotic danse macabre.
Such nonsense.

Whatever happened to my good luck?
So much for my black cat.

10 p.m.

After supper I stroll the summer strand,
sit silent on a fossil rock, and ponder
the Pleistocene. Then I watch the stars.

A heron stands silent on the shoreline
focusing the sharp stiletto of its beak –
a shadowy statue steadying itself
for a last stab at an evening snack.

Attention seeking

Shaded in the kitchen door
I sip an afternoon cup of tea
as my mind slips its moorings
and disappears out to sea . . .
A movement in the flowerbed
grabs my attention momentarily.

A blackbird (she who'd raised
a recent family of four fat chicks)
lies there spread-eagled.
Wings half unfurled,
brown beak agape, she makes
the slightest trembling on the soil.
The scene is worthy of Mimi
awaiting Rodolpho's aria:
"Your tiny hand is frozen."
(But no Rodolpho is in sight.)

I open the kitchen door, thinking
she's knackered or dying . . .
In a flash the trembling ceases,
she raises her head, swivels round
and gives me the eyeball.

Flustered flutterings ensue,
a cacophony of clucking. Then
one rumpled old bird of an artiste
flounces up into the air and trills off
over the fence and out of view.

La Stupenda!

The things you see

Beside Balcomie dump, among the bins,
stranger far than fiction, there they stood,
proud as only two peacocks could,
stepping through shrubs in late November sun,
their gorgeous blue-green feathers glinting,
haughty and hungry, looking for food,
but not begging for it.

That night I dreamt about them
strutting and shimmering in tropic heat,
pecking about some pampered peacock pen –
not shivering in a sharp east wind
beside a cold and grey North Sea,
and certainly not at the town dump,
grubbing about for their tea.

Winter ploughing, Kingsbarns

After John Masefield

Now that the root crops are all lifted in,
the weeds and shaws and plant remains lie dead.
The bonfire plumes burn the old season's leaves
and the countryside is looking sere and sad;

Now that the trees are naked and bereft,
and all the corn's been gathered into sheaves,
and stubble rows are all that's left to show,
and the northern hills carry their dusting of snow;

Now comes the tractor turning up the ground
and the dark soil glistering under a wintry sun
as screeching gulls follow, seeking grubs and fun;

Now the chill wind's behind as I wheel around
to admire the livid cerulean of the bay
and tell myself that spring's not far away.

Herons near Fife Ness

One, two, three, four:
the Cambo herons stand like sentries
all along Balcomie's cold and rocky shore.

Five, six, seven, eight:
the fishing can't be half bad
if they stand here morning, noon and late.

Grey and sleek and pointy
they never disappoint me.

Their cry? Raucous and coarse,
long throats a-croaking, rough and hoarse.

They loiter with intent
their fishy appetites to vent.

They're languid yet so focused
on their next meal, like the locust.

The privilege, the thrill
to watch them stand so very still.

Mankind, the moral midgets –
we are the frantic fidgets.

I stand and look upon a grey North Sea.
Bird-watching makes me hungry:
I fancy fish (with chips) for tea.

First hill of the year

Ben Tirran, Angus

A new year, new leaf, new hill . . .
as the year's first joyous lambs
frisk and spill over a sunny field.
I hear the young eagle's mewlings
and watch it yield to the high thermals
as I start my climb. Fat white hares
lope across a bracken-brown hillside,
bundles of moving conspicuousness.
A red grouse rises with loud cackle
to catapult from my feet at full throttle.

Spring warmth in the glen gives way
to the wind-bitten shock of an Arctic plateau
as Sunday walkers don jackets, hats, gloves,
and batten down. Long views compensate.
I pick out places I've been – the distant tops
of Dreish, Mayar, Mount Keen; and far
away and away – St Andrews Bay,
Fife Ness, even the pinprick Isle of May.

A new hill, new leaf, new year . . .
Even the foothills were a hard slog today
and up there the air felt thin and rare.
But still it was a good feeling to locate
then reach one's summit cairn at last.

A new year: what does the prospect show?
I try to walk around it, get the overview,
the outline of its likely peaks and dips.
But I can't – I must take my chances,
and I know I must go with the flow.

In the garden

Here I sit in the garden
watching summer plants grow.

I watch tadpoles swimming in their bowl,
growing up in the image of their kind.

I talk to blackbirds, sparrows, swallows
as they chat and flitter about.

I hear voices and footfalls from the lane
behind the garden wall: people being busy;

also bees buzzing in the buddleia
and zapping pollen from the peonies.

I soak up sunshine and a few spots of rain
on my arms, my face.

What a day: just enough time
to sit and stare, and make a rhyme.

I think about some of the stuff
I should be doing, and shrug shoulders.

How to round off this day? Perhaps
with a look at the sea, or grazing cows.

Overhead a plane drones in the heavens
and wants to send me indolent to sleep.

I contemplate the rigour of the world
and nod. Amen, hosanna.

A neighbour's death

Derry Jeffares, 1920–2005

I went to the newspaper as is my wont
to read the poem of the day,
but didn't yesterday. Instead I saw
his striking photograph and the obituary.

The photo captured a whiff of his spirit –
wise, generous, vibrant, convivial.
News of his death, whom I'd met so lately
arrested all my working day.

I wish we'd had more time
to discuss matters of mutual curiosity:
Crail, Yeats and Dublin for a start
and the whole business of making poetry.

Knowing him so briefly I had no expectancy
to hear in dream his Irish voice address me,
conversing in that gossipy, gleeful way
I'd so enjoyed at supper recently.

Will we imagine conversations like this
in times to come? Someone said
the dead we miss are easier to talk to.
Which is probably true, albeit sad.

I'm sure his death has intervened
in many lives. We who go on a while
will carry him along. Meanwhile,
I've still not read the poem of the day.

A winter's tale: the Crail whale and the Craighead rabbits

Remembering Jeanne Jeffares, 1921–2006

I first learn the tale of the Crail whale
on a Christmastime visit at Craighead Cottage.
Dr MacIntyre (the previous minister but one)
has called with his wife, and we sit chatting
with Mrs Jeffares. Here is the story.

The year is 1960, just after a national amnesty
for unregistered firearms. For some reason
in those days the minister of Crail has a gun.
So, duly and dutifully he registers the weapon
only to be told it's one of the biggest in the county.

About this time a large whale is washed up
on the Sauchope shore by an autumn storm.
The locals hope a high tide will float the whale
back out to sea. But the rocks hold it fast
and, plainly, it's becoming sore distressed.

The locals are worried and unhappy too,
conferring, wondering what's best to do
before deciding that the whale must be shot.
And – cometh the hour, cometh the man –
the minister is called upon to despatch it.

Picture the scene: a congregation processes
to the shore where the caravans now sit.
A sudden single shot from the famous gun
of large calibre puts the stranded mammal
beyond pain. No doubt a prayer is said.

•   •   •

Then (as stories tend to do) we skip a decade or two
and talk about the Crail constable. Like the minister,
he too is an excellent shot, and likes nothing better
than shooting a few fat rabbits for the pot
from the golf-links at Balcomie. A parenthesis:

Sometimes the constable mischievously claims
to be shooting lady golfers who, in those days
(like the rabbits), are becoming "too numerous
for their own good . . ." Here we are obliged
to visualise a none-too-PC PC . . . Easy.

During this period Mrs Jeffares is working hard
to establish her garden at Craighead. She fights
a mainly losing battle against marauding rabbits
as they gorge off her tasty rockery plants
and grow fat on her alpines and succulents.

The constable's offer to cull the vandals
is accepted with enthusiasm and gratitude,
and soon the garden is saved. In due course
from time to time, skinned and well boiled,
recycled rabbits are fed by Mrs Jeffares to her cats.

These are local-colour tales, stories among friends:
no easy way to round them off or point a moral
since they just go on, as we do.
All we can hope for is another chapter or two
another day, in the not too faraway.

Shag at bay

Wings outstretched, flailing into the gale
the black shag perches on his jet-black rock
among white waves, waiting for the wind to abate.

I'm walking the Caiplie shore as he pauses mid-flap
to check me out. I carry on along, and then look back,
pleased to see his flapping has resumed.

Picture the scene: the wind's scream, the sea's boom,
a grubby froth of spume daubing the shoreline,
him and me at the storm's vortex.

Then, scoured and cleansed I bend to the blast,
at last a sense of lightness to my step, my heart,
at this surreal elation of the elements.

The seals of Tay

On a sunny day
if the tide's at bay
the Tay seals like to lie
lolling on My Lord's Sandbank
under a summer sky.

From my commuter train
rattling across the bridge
I picture them in sun or rain
wearing sunglasses,
waving to pasty-faced passengers.

They're sleek and nicely plump,
with not a care in the world,
and I have to ask myself
who's fooling whom?
Are they laughing at us?

Pittenweem harbour

Today we rise to the challenge of the outer pier,
braced before the onset of an autumn storm
rehearsing for the real thing later in the year.

Sheltering from turbulence out at sea
a little auk bobs in the gentle swell
of the inner harbour, a dainty decoy.

(I checked him out in bird books: no neck
to speak of, this little comic is stubby of beak,
chubby of body, a winter visitor from the Arctic.)

We sprint the bad step half-way along the mole
buffeted by spindrift and flying seaweed
as spray from the waves smacks our faces.

From the pier-end light we watch the *Seaforth*
battle and roll her way towards the harbour's calm
across a choppy, gurly-growing firth.

Levelling with fishermen on the end of the pier
a crewman from the boat braves his dancing poop
to throw them a poly bag of live bait.

Then, faster than herring gulls the pier men swoop
for their bounty, as the bag bursts and spills
its grey-red mess of baby squid about their feet.

A pair of grey seals sweep the main channel
in the boat's wake, then raise big doggy heads,
sniff the wind, flip over, and follow it into port.

Fulmars at Crail

Two fulmars appeared last week
back from who knows where.
No fanfare, no fuss, no blare of publicity,
no twitchers' welcoming committee,
no one from the council, from welfare
or the churches . . . But there they were,
free aeronauts of the sea-fresh air,
their ledge on the sandstone cliff quite bare,
scoured squeaky clean below the Castle Walk
in the six months they've not been there.

I watch them glide stiff-winged across the bay
then ride the updrafts of an ocean gale. I cheer
quietly. Have they been with the fishing boats
or had a hard time of it farther north?
I love to hear their crooning grunts and cackles
and watch their bowings and head-shakings
as they take the time to greet a buddy.
I look forward with pleasant anticipation
to the proper setting-up of their seaside colony.

Fulmars are the only birds I can think of
that seem to fly for the sheer joy of it.
Elusive but sociable, they bother no one
unless invaded on their nesting patch.
But then, once disturbed an odd thing occurs
if you go too close. Shot from the nasal tubes
that lie along their beaks, you might receive
a squirt of stinking snot . . . I kid you not.

Black horse, lonely gannet, lame hare

He stands unmoving by the fence
too far inside his Highland field
for me to fetch his muzzle or haunch
a pat of fellow feeling or solidarity.
I never saw a sadder horse,
and in his stupor of sad apathy
he neither looks to left nor right.
He doesn't even paw the ground
but abject stares at lumps of grass
and fails to flick his mane or tail . . .

Another day, far from its Bass Rock colony
I never saw a lonelier gannet.
It stood upon Balcomie's empty shore,
head tucked tight under a furled wing,
now motionless, now twitching.
My calls and claps from the coastal path
were all ignored, so I left it to its thoughts.
Had it dived headlong once too often?
Been crossed in love? Bereaved? Whatever.
Like the black horse it chose to be alone . . .

Such creatures flash across my dreams
as if some outbreak of world weariness
is picking off the animal kingdom:
did my gannet make it through the night,
and did my black horse find the will to live?
What is it *like* to be an animal?
Sometimes we say it's hard to be a human
but on this anecdotal evidence
nor is it easy every livelong day
to be an equine or an avian.

As if for confirmation, another time
we follow the bottom field from Boarhills Farm
to Kittock's Den then down towards the sea,
starting a brown hare off its nest-like form
among the brittle stubble of the turf.
Its legs appear to fail it and it stops
to watch us from a distance of five yards,
crouching with clenched teeth.
I ponder survival chances for a lame hare
then shake my head at a fate so blatantly unfair.

Armistice Sunday, Crail

Two granite rows stand back to back for solidarity
behind the church in our town cemetery. Here lie
a score of young men and a Wren aged twenty-one
(a brief wife: "tread softly, my darling sleeps here").
One was a midshipman of nineteen. An airman died
four days before my birth. Almost all of them
were younger than my kids. The three Keeble boys,
killed in action in the Second War, are nearby
with their parents. They predeceased Grace,
their mother, by twenty empty years.

It's a quiet, sunny day with a background
of faint singing from the church. I stroll away
over empty fields inhaling long sea views.
Six roe deer freeze in mid-forage for winter grass,
their heads follow me, they watch me pass.
Here are harvest mice, herons and wrens (again!)
busy at their winter survival tasks. Partridges
whirr from the hedgerows into a safer distance.

I watch far-off matchstick men and women:
golfers bonding at their Sunday game,
farmers walking stubble fields, poking at their land,
families at play on a far-off silvery strand,
hikers with walking poles exploring coastal paths,
small boats in the bay, checking lobster-pots . . .
I pass the ruined wartime look-outs of Fife Ness
and the old airfield (noisy with car-racers today).

My father felt that we were the lucky ones,
for wasn't he spared the fate of an early grave,
of quitting the world as I was coming into it?
So true: despite cruel seas, Murmansk convoys,
Normandy landings and all the rest of it,
he came through . . . His message was simple:
"Always remember," he used to say.
I shall – and I do.

Two old bulls at Kinkell

For Jim Carruth

Transported out of the myths of Pict or Celt
they sit there at the mid-field,
two vast taureans chewing the fat,
a pair of chinless elder statesmen,
worldly wise jowls tilted towards each other,
jaw-jawing like warrior kings.

Sometimes the pair maintain a weather eye
on traffic up or down the road, but mainly
they just sit there. Once, cycling by
I heard a bovine sigh beneath the beech trees.
Calling across their dry-stone wall to them
I got a wary harrumph for sole reply.

In all the weathers known at Kinkell –
wind, wet, sleet or the hot sun's magic spell –
the twosome sit pondering in their pomp.
The one, a sleekly massive, black-sheened bull
with silly, short-clipped horns,
sports a look of spaced-out regal hugeness.

The other is his impassive Highland cousin
of the matted, Hey-Jimmy dreadlocks
and wide-splayed, lethal pronghorns –
to say nothing of the golden nose-ring
or the wee-bit radgy, soople, slittery air
of wha daur meddle wi me.

Is that the wisp of a smile
flickering across the black bull's patriarch face
as he remembers his prime in another place –
all that summer fuss and nonsense long ago
(loudspeakers, pipe bands, gleaming machines)
when he won gold at the Fife Agricultural Show?

Unkempt but warm under his mucky coat,
what are Hey-Jimmy's winter dreams?
Is he ruminating back to halcyon days
among skittish heifers and dozy cows
that could barely stand his weight
when he was the uncontested stud of Glen Clova?

A man passing through

Thank you for these days
and for this book of days.
It shows me where I've been
and bits of what I've seen.
It helps me make some sense
as I begin to venture hence.
It tells me what and who I loved
ere I was old, hatted or gloved.

Thank you for all the ways
you've given me to fill my days;
for granting me good health
to keep some wits and stealth;
for lending me this hearth, this fire,
to sit and read by when I tire;
for helping me keep faith
while I've been drawing breath.

And though I've never worked God out
or made too much to shout about,
yesterday walking up the glen
I grasped the gist of it again.
So thank you for keeping me
from drifting too far out to sea,
and thank you for peace of mind
in spite of humankind.

Harbour scene, St Andrews

Hunched into a cold easterly
I stand on the footbridge at the Shorehead
and scan the outer harbour, the choppy sea.

Hurrying past comes a lady from the RSPB
with a clumsy bundle in her arms
happed up in a grubby old towel.

Now I see the cygnet's dull grey cowl
swaying on the end of a snake-like neck
from left to right: an ungainly metronome.

Gently, the lady places her load by the slipway
beneath my feet. We stand there and it looks at me.
Together we contemplate a choppy greenish sea.

"They were causing a serious obstruction
for shoppers at Morrison's car-park.
No sign of the parents, need I mention . . .

"So we lifted them, after a customer's objection.
As of now, they're on probation. Next time
they'll get an antisocial behaviour order."

She bustles away, soon to return with a sibling,
placing it by the first bird. Then, they and I
all three watch choppy sea and stormy sky.

"Go on," I say to them. "Try the water."
And gingerly, defiantly, elegantly,
the two wee tearaways launch themselves.

The resident mute-swan flotilla then appears
in full-sail splendour from the inner harbour:
two nebby adults and six cygnets billowing along.

These young are nearly adult, their grey feathers
flecked with white. They are all bigger by far
than the two delinquents. So, peace or war?

In the hiss and snort of a near-mute, watch-it welcome
the two tearaways tread water in shock and awe:
ten necks and heads then nod, kiss and caress.

Such breeding, such tact, such authority
from the strapping residents: such finesse!

Planting late bulbs

I thought we'd planted – or re-planted –
all our bulbs some weeks ago. Not so,
for yesterday I found a tray of hyacinths
and tulips to remind me that we'd still a bit to do.

They'd started sprouting pale-green waxy nodes
in their impatience, their imperative to grow.
But they lay outwith their element, all arrested,
and now the forecast was for snow.

This morning saw a brief lull in the weather
as the west wind ceased to howl and blow.
So into dark garden soil they went at last, and now
they're getting ready for another season's show.

I wanted to apologise to them, say sorry
that they'd almost missed the boat . . . I know
that we'd have missed the blaze of next year's tulips
and the hyacinths' blue-scented glow.

Another Remembrance Day, near Crail

This autumn day, soft, damp and still,
I walk the shore from Cambo till
by Randerston a full tide forces me to walk
the clifftops, clambering across loose rock.

I look down a lush and sloping cowfield
to watch as silent herons creep uphill
among chomping cattle: quite comical.
They seem to think they are invisible.

I skirt a pungent dewy field, knee-high
with mid-November, blue-green broccoli
readying itself for Christmas dinnerplates.

Goldfinches in a chattering charm
(red, yellow, black, white) and a chitting swarm
of yellowhammers (citron and chestnut-brown)
are sporting across this silent sea of brassica.

I sclim over a mossy boundary wall
into a huge stubble field. Exploding into the mist
flocks of partridges crik-crik away in a whirr
of reddish dumpy tails, beating retreat.

Suddenly, midfield, eight roe-deer rise as one.
Circus-like, they circle the bare field's perimeter
in a wide and unpredictable run-around.

I recall these friends: partridges, finches, deer
I stood and watched in this place, at this time, last year.

Cold snap

We'd planned a walk up Glen Prosen
but couldn't go: it was frozen.
So we went to Montrose
where we froze.

Too cold for fun
at the House of Dun,
too cold in truth
to stop off at Arbroath,
too cold to be naughty
at Broughty; while Lunan Bay
was battleship grey, and Monifieth
was chattering teeth.

Our cheeks and noses
were bright red roses
so we stopped at Dundee
for toast and tea.

You know what they say,
said my frost-nipped wife:
A day out of Crail
is a day out of life.
So then we turned tail
and fled home to Fife.

Where we *immediately* put a fire on.
Home is where the hearth is,
it ain't so cold there.

Air miles, flying south

For Mike Erskine

They were flying high, flying fast,
flying noisy as they passed
across the early-morning bustle
of Crail High Street.

We all stopped to look up
and the little boy said, "What is it Dad?"
Dad said, "It's the geese,
they're on a mission."

And we all kept looking up:
the greengrocer outside his shop
with a tray of soft fruit in his arms;
an old lady getting carefully into her car;
the minister precarious on his bike;
a hassled, perspiring delivery man
unloading crates from the Co-op van;
youngsters dawdling schoolwards
killing time, kicking a can . . .

while the racket of overhead debate
flew on: "Come on, keep up, we're late!"
Or, "Let's fly a bit to left (or right)."
Or, "Who's in charge of this flight?"

And then the geese were gone
weaving south in sinuous skeins,
focused on far-off feeding grounds,
leaving us standing. Wondering.

The road, the miles

Victoria Hospital, Kirkcaldy

The ward is waking up,
a trolley squeaks along.
This is an early-morning song . . .

A mild stroke, the doctor said
and sorrowfully shook his head.
If that was a mild one – well,
please God protect me
from anything more challenging
on the Richter scale.

I still see, more or less.
I still stand straight-ish, tall-ish.
I still feel joy and sorrow.
Hallelujah, I've had a stroke
and I ain't about to go up in smoke.
I still just about relish a joke.

But I lie here vaguely thinking
of the view from the ambulance, looking
back along the road, the miles
I've come to reach this point, the life
I've lived to bring me to this place,
this weary sadness in a doctor's face.

Kenspeckle man

Minding Duncan Glen, 1933–2008

Alas, anither licht's gaed dim
athort wir Scottish stage:
Duncan, wha helpt his peers I hymn
fae this tae the neist age.

Teacher, bukeman, makar, penter –
Duncan *wis* the Akros Press,
imprent o unique distinction,
staunin weel abune the rest.

A year back I wis chairmed be Duncan
askin me fur "a wee buke"[1].
When I speirt at whit tae gie him,
he said poems fae the East Neuk.

Sune I'd makkit a disk tae send him;
page pruifs cam back be return.
Then he sayd we needit photies:
the canty snappin wis braw fun

at herbours (Ainster an Pittenweem),
kirkyairds (Crail an Carnbee),
castles (Kellie an Balcomie),
an ferms aside the ayeweys flichterin sea.

Sinsyne the wee buke coalesced
three months efter thon request.
So thanks, auld freend, fur mindin me
whit joy the halesome ploy can be.

An thank ye fur encouragement,
a thingmy aye in short supply.
Ye gied a helping haun tae ithers.
Duncan, we salute ye as we say guid-bye.

1 The wee buke was *Poems Mainly from the East Neuk, Fife* (Akros, 2007), one of the last
titles issued under Duncan's distinguished imprint. Now out of print, it was the direct
forerunner of the present publication.

High noon, Crail?

High noon under an azure sky.
Their ghetto-blaster splits the salt-sea air
as three young strangers hit the town,
one with a Charles Bronson moustache
straight out of *Once Upon a Time in the West*.

They swagger up Crail's empty High Street,
the bees' knees, masters of all they survey –
cowboys heading for the shootout
outside the Golf Hotel maybe
with a posse of our local hardmen?

They disappear into Barnett's, the bakers,
and re-emerge with pies, doughnuts, tea.

Snaw scenes, East Fife

Things no seen
at Kenly Green –

snawy spoor
on Magus Muir,

roe deer foraging fer food
steppin doon bi Cambo Wuid

as aince agane the warld gaes chill
an spindrift flees aff Lucklaw Hill.

Noo the sun's striking Kittock's Den.
We step through trees, an then – an then –

there's snaw ower the Sidlaws
an sun ower the sea.

High tide's at Kinshaldy
an here's whaur I'd be.

Sune eneuch'll come the thaw
creepin ower Kellie Law.

Kellie Castle garden

The year's first ladybird
appears in Kellie Castle garden
on 18th March, a mild and softish day.

On a serrated leaf of hellebore
she walks the walk
in her red spotted frock.

"Oh look at her," I say.
"Well spotted," you reply,
"if you'll allow the pun."

The cawing rooks are racketing
on still-bare trees in the westering sun.
Only the deaf can make such dins.

Plum trees are flowering pinkish gins
while sticky pink foreskins
of rhubarb stretch their stomata
as they prepare to penetrate warm air.
The heady smell of spring is almost there.

Someone has painted gates and seats,
dug soil and swept the winter back,
brushed down bee skeps in readiness.
The place looks good,
all set for growth, for fruitfulness.

There's a feeling of anticipation
with every greening braird in bud.
You can smell the box hedge.
Fluting blackbirds warble from the lawns.
Another summer beckons.

Deer stalking

As I walk up Kirklands today
the wind is from the west,
spring ploughing under way.

Tiny blips dot the skyline
of the top field towards Wormiston
and I know they're observing me.

Two stand, the rest sit watching
while I detour round by the trees,
trying to drop from their view.

Wind noise and direction in my favour,
they neither hear nor smell me
from the copse as I close in.

Ah but a twig snaps and they stand
as one to look my way, then hightail it
down the field, seven winking scuts.

Not to risk a barbed-wire fence
they circle down to another copse.
Again, for a minute they're out of view.

Then they're in the field beyond,
running uphill towards a windy skyline
and over it – over and out.

Half an hour later, another field away
five of them head for Randerston.
They must have jumped the big stone wall.

Last sighting: the other two
shoot across my path behind Balcomie
only to merge into brown ploughland.

These two had only been ten yards away –
the wall had been too high for them.
Brief joy to share some space with them.

Hurdy-gurdy man, Ainster

There he stauns bi the pierheid
an ca's the wheel o "The Nor Wund",
birlin its shiny bress haunle
an gien his "Queen o Barrel Organs" laldie.

A sma thrang o us sit alang the herbour wa
shooglin an dingin time wi joco feet
on skirie cobblestanes. Ower us a'
an August sun gies walcome heat.

Kids an grown fowk too are gled
tae thraw thir coins intil his bawbee-boax,
an pose wi hurdy-gurdy man for photiegraphs.
Mensefu tae yin an a' he smiles, raises his hat.

Een hauf-shut i' the sklent sheeny sun
we lik fine the auld-time lilts an tunes –
an jalouse wirsels in doontoon Bruges
or mibbe the Vondel Pairk in Amsterdam.

Walkin the dug

Ane mair bend
alang the pend
road end

ower the pairk
i the hauf derk
dugs berserk

stroll thonder
tak a daunder
time tae ponder

hip hap
twist an stap
jimp an flap

fash the ba'
loup the wa'
tak a fa'

boo hoo
get yer poo
whaurivver noo

•   •   •

Twinklin still
starn bleeze an spill
ahint the hill

wabbit eyes
wun the prize
o birlin, dancin skies

nae wirry
whit's yer hurry
exemplary

Tammie-Norrie

*Fer Pam an Colin Mitchell, minding a braw day
on the Isle o May*

A Tammie-Norrie's uniform
is fedders bleck an white.
Its neb is monie-coloured,
its dumpy orange legs is bright.

"Puffin" is its Sabbath nem.
Some chiels cry it "sea-parrot".
A wheen o glaikit folk wull claim
its nem is "bottleneb". Scunner on thaim!

"Norrie" is the craitur's Shetland nem
wi "Tammie" added on oot o affection.
He weirs his dooble-barrel athoot shame –
methinks it suits the wee burd tae perfection.

Mist ower the May i the heat o June
an the fermers win the hairst richt sune,
file Tammie-Norrie o the May
dooks in the sea the lee-lang day.

Swairms o Norries lik bumbees bizz
alang the cliff-heuchs – hark at thir fizz.
But Tammie-Norrie o the Bass
daurna kiss a bonnie lass.

Fae nor-Atlantic seas they fly
tae find thir wee bit grund that's dry.
Then Tammie-Norrie o Inchkeith
wull howk his burrae underneath

sea-grass an soorocks, lichen an scree: *soorocks*, sorrel
here's whaur he maks a nest, ye see.
The feck o Norries mate fer life,   *feck*, majority
tae raise thir puffling, him an the wife.   *puffling*, baby puffin

An file Norrie o the May
catches sand-eels ivvrie day,
Norrie o the Bass
feeds his puffling neath sea-grass.

One chook a year is mair nor eneuch
tae feed wi sand-eels an sic-like stuff,
tae scug fae seagulls an muckle seas: *scug*, protect, hide
thon's thir challenge, gin ye please.

But thae wee burds aye keep the heid,
they nivver cheep aboot thir loasses.
Richt at life's edge they tak thir breid
nor beck tae ony fantoosh bosses.   *fantoosh*, fancy, flashy

An here's the thing.

Life's clowns have aye a serious face
an Tammie's nae exception.
Lik awbody wha'd entertain the human race,
he ettles whiles tae practise introspection.

Sabbath

The town's church bell goes ding-a-ling
across the quiet morning, speaking
to those who like that sort of thing.

I am lying low, nearer God's work here
behind the wall in this patch of garden.
Sotto voce, here I also sing.

Squatting, I cut back papery brown heads
among the silence of last year's hydrangeas –
pruning, tidying, that sort of thing.

Blue-green snowdrop spears are pushing through,
early grape hyacinths and crocus too.
Quite soon it will be spring.

Cold contempt for crocuses

Latterly, she registered raw fury
at the merest glimpse of crocuses.
I wondered at the fierce contempt,
the pent-up anathema they aroused from her.
What harm did crocuses ever do?

She was in her late eighties
when I asked her the question once,
after a memorable outburst beside a bonnie bed
of them. And what did she say
on that otherwise fine spring day?

"Huh!" she denounced them. "Nae sooner here
than wede awa'! They war coming oot last week,
and luik at them noo: feenished!"
Aweel, she was just railing against her destiny,
which was much the same as theirs, or mine.

Later on, a penny drops. "Fair daffodils,
we weep to see you haste away so soon . . ."
It's true; in crocuses as in daffodils we see
intimations and markers of our own mortality,
and we are troubled by the sight.

On the wisdom of acquiring a dog at seventy

Argument

I need an occupation for today
to take my mind away from idleness.
I do not want my life to drift away
or let my brain seek peace through emptiness.

So give me a project that will stretch my skills –
down-to-earth and practical, no frills.
I need a focus to disperse all mental fog.
I need a dog.

Counter-argument

"Now is that wise?" I think I hear you say.
"If dogs arrive, they tend to stay . . . and stay.
They trash your garden, wet the kitchen floor,
and (when your back is turned) flee out the door.

"They love to interrupt you when you talk,
and rain or shine they *always* need their walk.
They're nought but grief, forby endless expense –
a dog for you at your age makes no sense."

Outcome (one week later)

We got one anyway,
a cocker spaniel pup from Kingsbarns, yesterday.
The house is a shambles, it's been through the blitz.
The puppy's called Brodie, we love it to bits.

Well, that's the "official" line, but watch this space.
Soon I may eat humble pie, accepting loss of face
as I look at tulips trampled, at daffodils destroyed,
at poor flowerbeds flattened – and *refuse* to get annoyed.

So far.